Symbols of Canada

Coats of Arms

Edited by Deborah Lambert

Weigl

Published by Weigl Educational Publishers Limited
6325 10 Street SE
Calgary, Alberta
T2H 2Z9

www.weigl.com

Library and Archives Canada Cataloguing in Publication data available upon request.
Fax 403-233-7769 for the attention of the Publishing Records department.

ISBN 978-1-55388-922-9 (hard cover)
ISBN 978-1-55388-928-1 (soft cover)

Printed in the United States of America
1 2 3 4 5 6 7 8 9 0 13 12 11 10 09

Editor: Heather C. Hudak
Design: Kathryn Livingstone

All of the Internet URLs given in the book were valid at the time of publication. However, due to the dynamic nature
of the Internet, some addresses may have changed, or sites may have ceased to exist since publication. While the author
and publisher regret any inconvenience this may cause readers, no responsibility for any such changes can be accepted
by either the author or the publisher.

Every reasonable effort has been made to trace ownership and to obtain permission to reprint copyright material. The publishers
would be pleased to have any errors or omissions brought to their attention so that they may be corrected in subsequent printings.

Weigl acknowledges Getty Images as one of its primary image suppliers for this title.
Alamy: pages 4, 24 right; Government of Alberta: pages 10, 23; Government of Nunavut: pages 17, 23; Government of Ontario™:
pages 18, 23; Government of PEI Executive Council: pages 19, 23; Gouvernement du Québec: pages 20, 23; Government of
Saskatchewan Protocol Dept.: pages 21, 23, 28: Newfoundland and Labrador Provincial Government Policy and Planning Division:
pages 14, 23; Province of Manitoba: pages 12, 23; ©Province of Nova Scotia, Communications Nova Scotia, Creative Services: pages
16, 23; Provincial Government of British Columbia: pages 11, 23; Provincial Government of New Brunswick: pages 13, 23;
Reproduction authorized by the Library of Parliament/Reproduction autorisée par la Bibliothèque du Parlement: pages 23, 26, and 27;
Territorial Government of the Northwest Territories: pages 15, 23; Territorial Government of the Yukon: pages 22, 23.

We gratefully acknowledge the financial support of the Government of Canada through the Book Publishing Industry Development
Program (BPIDP) for our publishing activities.

Contents

Ontario

Northwest Territories

Saskatchewan

Prince Edward Island

Nunavut

Quebec

Yukon

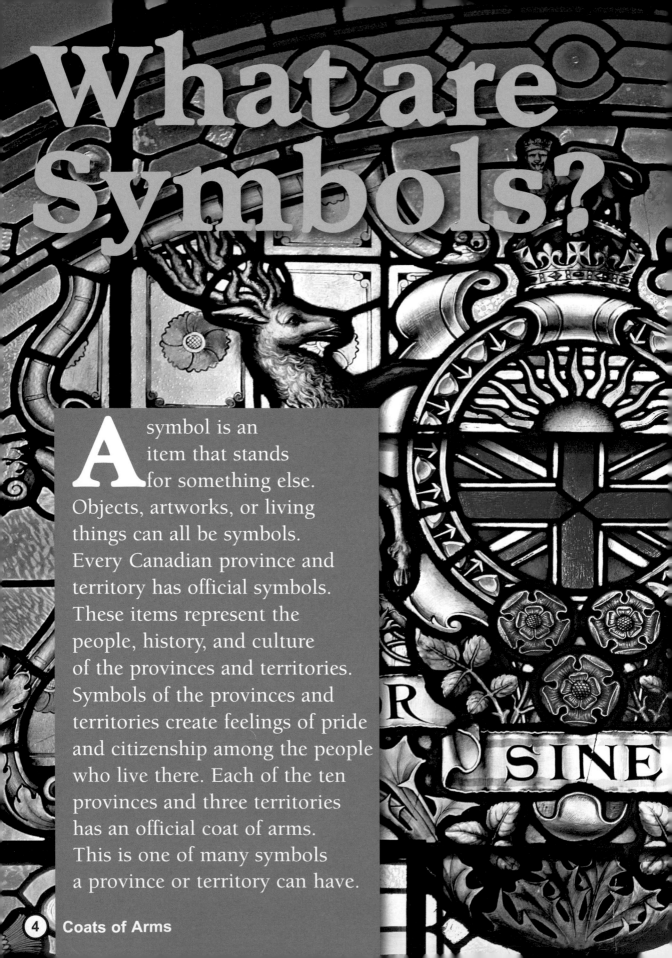

What are Symbols?

A symbol is an item that stands for something else. Objects, artworks, or living things can all be symbols. Every Canadian province and territory has official symbols. These items represent the people, history, and culture of the provinces and territories. Symbols of the provinces and territories create feelings of pride and citizenship among the people who live there. Each of the ten provinces and three territories has an official coat of arms. This is one of many symbols a province or territory can have.

Creating a Coat of Arms

A coat of arms is a special design that represents a group or a region. Often, it is drawn on or around a **shield**. Nations have been using coats of arms since ancient times. They often were used by knights on their shields as a way to tell **allies** from enemies. In Great Britain, arms were created for individuals and passed from father to son, and mother to daughter, to show social status. However, because coats of arms could only be used by one person at a time, they were changed in some way to represent the new bearer. Today, countries, individuals, and businesses all over the world have coats of arms. In Canada, the country, as well as each province and territory, has a coat of arms to honour their **heritage**.

Knights' shields often were decorated with a coat of arms.

Locating Provinces and Territories

Yukon

Northwest Territories

Nunavut

British Columbia

Alberta

Saskatchewan

Manitoba

Each province and territory has a coat of arms. Each province and territory is unique because of its land, people, and wildlife. Throughout this book, the provinces and regions are colour coded. To find a coat of arms, first find the province or territory using the map on this page. Then, turn to the pages that have the same colour province or territory image in the top corner.

Web Crawler

Find out facts about each province and territory at **http://canada.gc.ca/othergov-autregouv/prov-eng.html**. Click on each province and territory.

Newfoundland and Labrador

Quebec

Prince Edward Island

Ontario

Nova Scotia

New Brunswick

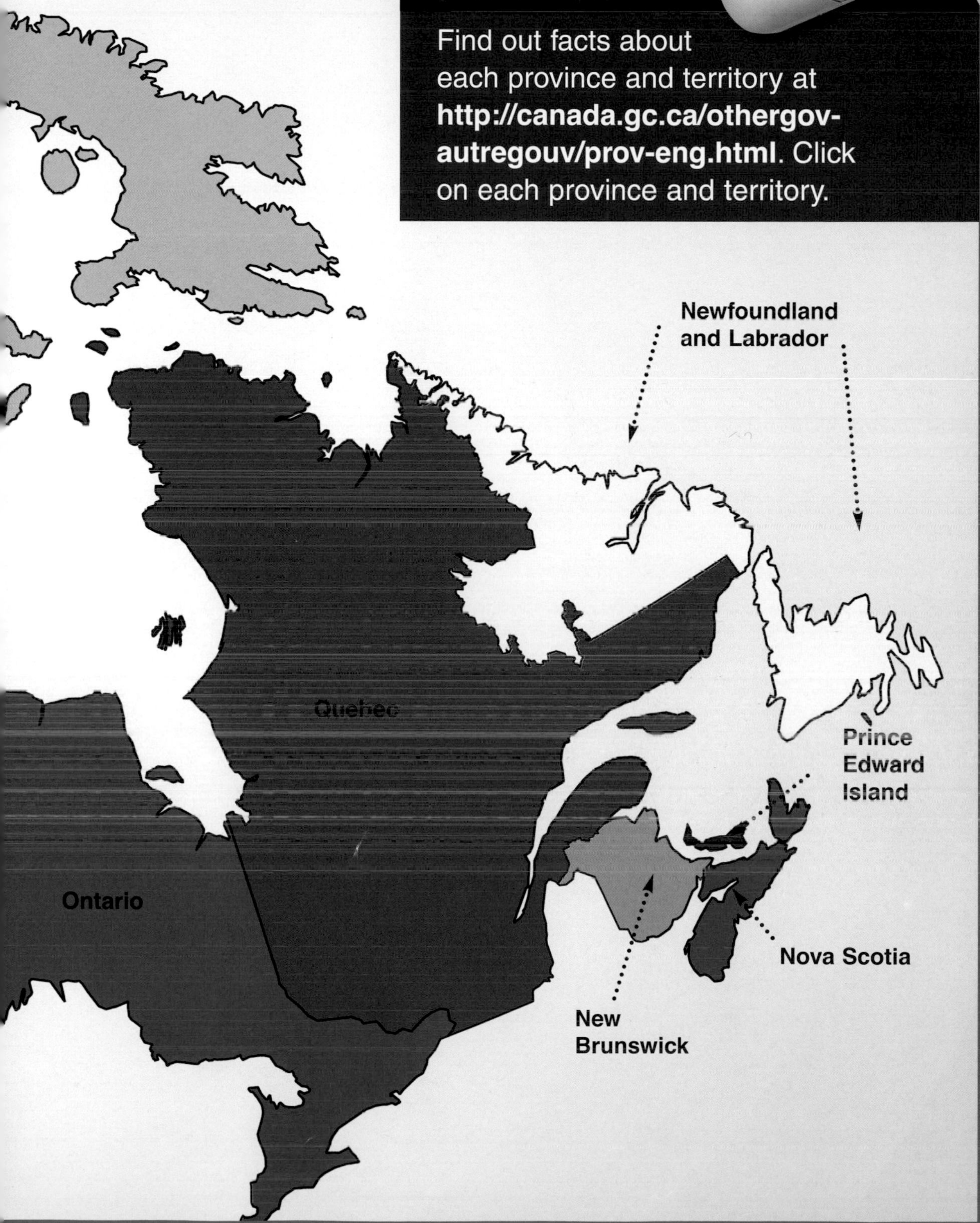

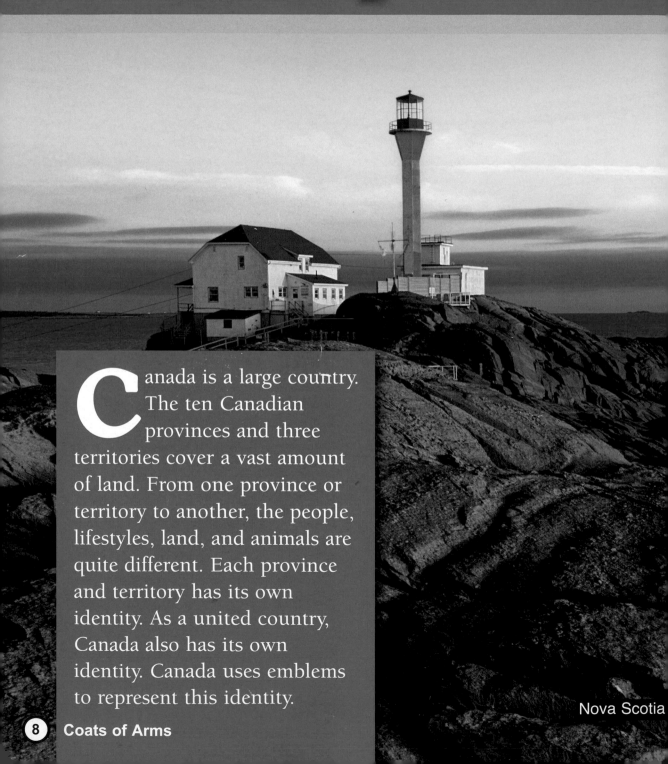

Canada's Land and People

Canada is a large country. The ten Canadian provinces and three territories cover a vast amount of land. From one province or territory to another, the people, lifestyles, land, and animals are quite different. Each province and territory has its own identity. As a united country, Canada also has its own identity. Canada uses emblems to represent this identity.

Nova Scotia

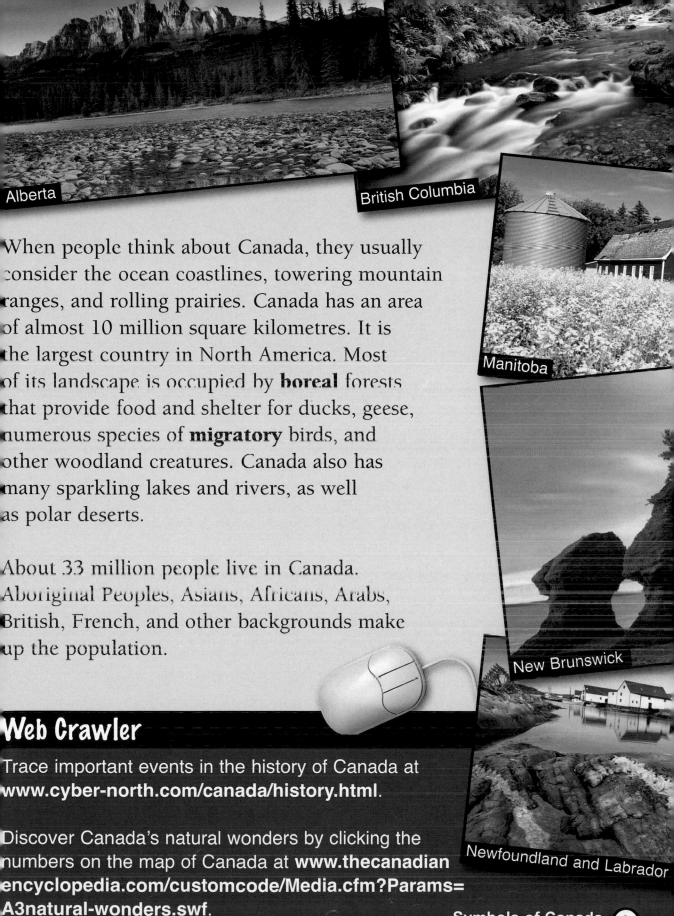

Alberta

British Columbia

Manitoba

When people think about Canada, they usually consider the ocean coastlines, towering mountain ranges, and rolling prairies. Canada has an area of almost 10 million square kilometres. It is the largest country in North America. Most of its landscape is occupied by **boreal** forests that provide food and shelter for ducks, geese, numerous species of **migratory** birds, and other woodland creatures. Canada also has many sparkling lakes and rivers, as well as polar deserts.

About 33 million people live in Canada. Aboriginal Peoples, Asians, Africans, Arabs, British, French, and other backgrounds make up the population.

New Brunswick

Web Crawler

Trace important events in the history of Canada at **www.cyber-north.com/canada/history.html**.

Discover Canada's natural wonders by clicking the numbers on the map of Canada at **www.thecanadian encyclopedia.com/customcode/Media.cfm?Params= A3natural-wonders.swf**.

Newfoundland and Labrador

Alberta

Alberta's coat of arms was officially granted to the province by King Edward VII on May 30, 1907. In 1980, a crest, supporters, and a motto were added to the shield to form the province's present coat of arms.

At the top of the coat of arms, there is a royal crown that represents Canada's ties to the British **monarchy**. Beneath the crown, a beaver rests upon a red and white wreath. The beaver stands for the fur trade that led to the exploration and settlement of Alberta and Canada. At the top of the shield, there is a red cross on a white background. Known as St. George's Cross, it stands for Alberta's traditional ties to Great Britain.

Images of foothills, mountains, prairies, and wheat fields symbolize Alberta's many landscapes. The antelope represents Alberta's abundant wildlife, and the lion stands for Great Britain. Alberta's official flower emblem, wild roses, lie beneath the lion and the antelope. They grow naturally in many parts of the province. Alberta's motto, *Fortis et Liber*, Latin for "Strong and Free," is written beneath the roses.

British Columbia

British Columbia's coat of arms was granted to the province by King Edward VII in 1906. The crest, supporters, and motto were added to the shield by Queen Elizabeth II on October 15, 1987.

The coat of arms has a lion standing on a crown that represents the **Royal Crest**. The lion wears a collar of Pacific dogwood flowers, British Columbia's official flower. Beneath the crown, a wreath sits on a gold helmet. Great Britain's flag, the Union Jack, is on the top half of the shield. The flag represents British Columbia's past as a **colony** of Great Britain.

On the bottom part of the shield, wavy blue and silver bars and a setting Sun represent British Columbia's location between the Pacific Ocean and the Rocky Mountains. On either side of the coat of arms stand a stag and ram. They represent the early colonies of British Columbia and Vancouver Island. The wreath and banner beneath the Royal Crest are red and white, the official colours of Canada. Dogwood flowers encircle British Columbia's Latin motto, *Splendor Sine Occasu*, which means "Splendour Without Diminishment."

Manitoba

Manitoba's coat of arms was officially granted to the province by King Edward VII on May 10, 1905.

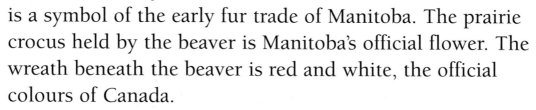

A royal crown sits above a beaver at the top of the coat of arms. The crown represents Manitoba's heritage as part of the British monarchy. The beaver is a symbol of the early fur trade of Manitoba. The prairie crocus held by the beaver is Manitoba's official flower. The wreath beneath the beaver is red and white, the official colours of Canada.

St. George's Cross, on the top part of the shield, represents King George III and the province's British heritage. Under the cross, a bison is shown to represent the vast herds that once roamed throughout the province. On either side of the shield, a unicorn and a horse stand on a base of water, wheat fields, and forests. The unicorn represents Manitoba's early Scottish settlers. The horse is an important animal to **First Nations**, the Métis, and European settlers. Manitoba's Latin motto, *Gloriosus et Liber*, which means "Glorious and Free," is written on a ribbon that wraps around the base of the coat of arms.

New Brunswick

Queen Victoria approved New Brunswick's original coat of arms in 1868. To celebrate New Brunswick's 200th anniversary, in 1984, Queen Elizabeth II granted the crest and supporters, and confirmed the motto.

The gold lion on the shield of the coat of arms connects the province to the British royal family. A ship with moving oars beneath the lion represents the province's shipping past. The blue wavy lines below the ship link the province to the sea. Two white-tailed deer on either side of the shield have crests hanging from their collars. One crest is the Union Jack, a symbol of Great Britain. The other crest is the fleur-de-lis. In French, *fleur* means "flower," and *lis* means "lily." This **stylized** lily is a symbol of France.

Fiddleheads, or the leaves of a young fern, are shown growing below the deer's feet. Fiddleheads are a New Brunswick delicacy. These ferns are boiled and served with lemon and butter. Beside the fiddleheads are purple violets, New Brunswick's provincial flower. At the bottom of the coat of arms is the Latin phrase *Spem Reduxit*, which means "Hope was restored."

Newfoundland and Labrador

Newfoundland and Labrador's coat of arms is one of the oldest in Canada and was originally used by a private company. It was introduced by King Charles I of England in 1637. By 1928, the coat of arms was officially adopted by the province.

Some people believe the elk on top of the shield was meant to be a caribou since elk do not live in Newfoundland and Labrador. Two Beothuk warriors hold the shield. The Beothuk lived in Newfoundland when Europeans first arrived. They represent Newfoundland and Labrador's heritage and the first people. By the mid-1800s, the Beothuk no longer existed.

Two lions and two unicorns decorate the shield. These animals represent the province's ties to England and Scotland. The red and silver colours on the shield symbolize Saint John the Baptist. John Cabot discovered Newfoundland on the Feast Day of St. John the Baptist. The scroll at the base of the shield is inscribed with the province's motto *Quaerite Prime Regnum Dei*, which is Latin for "Seek Ye First the Kingdom of God."

Northwest Territories

The Northwest Territories' coat of arms is found in the centre of the territory's official seal. It was approved by Queen Elizabeth II on February 7, 1957. Each part of its design stands for a certain aspect of life in the North.

The coat of arms has two narwhals that face outward and protect a compass rose. The compass rose symbolizes the magnetic North Pole. The narwhals and compass rose rest on a red and white wreath.

The upper part of the shield is white with a jagged base. White represents the territory's polar ice. The wavy blue line symbolizes the Northwest Passage. This passage is a waterway that connects the Atlantic and Pacific Oceans.

The lower part of the shield is divided by a black diagonal line into red and green sections. The red represents **tundra** that makes up the northern parts of the territory. The white fox's head represents the fur of the many animals found in the area. The green stands for the forests found in the southern parts of the territory, while the gold bars symbolize minerals.

Nova Scotia

Nova Scotia's coat of arms is the oldest in Canada. It was adopted by the province in 1625 and honours the province's Scottish heritage.

A banner with Nova Scotia's motto is written in Latin at the top of the coat of arms. It reads *Munit Haec et Altera Vincit*, which means "One defends and the other conquers." Beneath the banner are two joined hands holding a laurel and thistle. The laurel is a symbol of peace, and the thistle is a symbol of Scotland. On either side of the coat of arms is a unicorn and an Aboriginal person. The unicorn and its crowns represent Nova Scotia's past as a British colony. The Aboriginal person is a symbol of Nova Scotia's first inhabitants.

Nova Scotia's shield of arms lies in the centre of the coat of arms. The shield is white with a blue "X" across the centre. The "X" stands for the Cross of Saint Andrew, the patron saint of Scotland. The Royal Lion, a symbol of Scottish royalty, is in the centre of the Cross of Saint Andrew. A Scottish thistle and mayflowers are below the shield. Mayflowers, the official flowers of Nova Scotia, were added to the coat of arms in 1929.

Nunavut

Nunavut's coat of arms is known as The Arms of Her Majesty in Right of Nunavut. The right to use the coat of arms was granted by Roméo Leblanc, Governor-General of Canada, on April 1, 1999, one day before Nunavut became an official territory.

The igloo at the top of the coat of arms represents the Inuit's traditional way of life. The crown symbolizes Nunavut's inclusion in **Confederation**. On either side of the coat of arms stands a *tuktu*, or caribou, and *qilalugaq tugaalik*, or narwhal. They represent the Inuit's reliance on the land and sea for their survival.

In the centre of the coat of arms is a circle divided into blue and gold portions. These colours represent the riches of the land, ocean, and sky. The star in the blue part of the shield symbolizes how the elders guide the people. The circles show the life-giving properties of the Sun. An **inukshuk** in the gold part of the shield guides people on land and marks special places. The **qulliq** stands for light and the warmth of family and community. Beneath the shield, Nunavut's motto *Nunavut Sanginivut*, or "Nunavut, Our Strength," is written in Inuktitut.

Ontario

Ontario's coat of arms was created in 1868. The animals on either side of the shield and the crest above the shield were added to the design in 1909. Ontario's coat of arms has been stylized since it was created.

VT INCEPIT   SIC PERMANET

FIDELIS

At the top of the design, a black bear stands on a green and gold wreath. The bear represents the abundance of Ontario's varied wildlife. On either side of the coat of arms, there is a moose and a deer. These animals have lived in Ontario for thousands of years.

Between the animals and beneath the wreath is the shield. The top of the shield shows the Cross of St. George. This cross represents the British heritage of many people in Ontario. It also honours King George III, who ruled the colony when the shield was created. Three golden maple leaves on a green background represent the common maple trees found in the province. A banner with the province's motto flows beneath the shield and animals. The motto, *Ut incepit Fidelis sic permanet*, is Latin for "Loyal She Began and Loyal She Remains."

Prince Edward Island

Prince Edward Island's coat of arms is linked to its past as a British colony. King Edward VII gave the province its coat of arms on May 30, 1905. The design changed in 2002.

At the top of the coat of arms, a blue jay stands upon a small mound of grass, holding an oak leaf in its beak. The blue jay is the official bird of Prince Edward Island. The golden helmet beneath the red and white wreath represents the role the province has played in Confederation. Silver foxes on either side of the coat of arms symbolize the hard-working, clever people of the province.

A lion, a symbol of Great Britain, is on the top part of the shield. The three oak saplings represent the three counties of Prince Edward Island—Kings County, Queens County, and Prince County. The oak tree is another symbol of Great Britain. Beneath the shield is an eight-point star, a symbol used by the **Mi'kmaq** people to represent the Sun. Lady's slippers surround the star. They represent early European settlers and are the official floral emblem of Prince Edward Island. At the bottom of the coat of arms is the motto *Parva sub Ingenti*, Latin for "The Small Under the Protection of the Great."

Quebec

Quebec's coat of arms recognizes both England and France and was approved in 1868, just after Confederation. In 1939, the Quebec government updated its design to highlight the history and heritage of the province.

In the design of the coat of arms, the French crown sits above the shield. The fleur-de-lis, a symbol of France, represents Quebec's strong ties to France. Beneath the crown is the shield.

This shield is divided into three parts. The top part displays three fleurs-de-lis on a blue background. The middle part shows a gold lion with a blue tongue and claws. The lion represents Great Britain. The bottom part displays three green maple leaves on a gold background. The maple leaf has been a symbol of Canada for almost 200 years. The maple tree is common in Quebec, and its green colour represents the province.

Beneath the shield is a banner with the province's motto *Je me souviens*, French for "I remember." Many people think the motto is meant to remind French Canadians of their French heritage and to preserve their culture.

Saskatchewan

Saskatchewan's coat of arms, which symbolizes the province's

prairie heritage, was approved by Queen Elizabeth II on September 16, 1986. Then, it only had a shield of arms. In 1906, King Edward VII approved the shield's use in the present design of the province's coat of arms.

Canada's national animal, the beaver, appears above a wreath of red and white, Canada's national colours. The beaver holds a western red lily and wears a golden crown. The crown is a symbol of the province's connection to the British monarchy.

On either side of the coat of arms stand a lion and white-tailed deer wearing beadwork that honours the Aboriginal Peoples of Saskatchewan. A red royal lion occupies the top part of the shield. Three golden sheaves of wheat on a green background are displayed on the bottom part of the shield. The green represents forests and grass. Red is for the western red lily, and brown stands for farming. Western red lilies support a scroll inscribed with the motto, *Multis E Gentibus Vires*, Latin for "From Many Peoples Strength."

Yukon

The Yukon's coat of arms, which honours the territory's northern heritage, was designed by Alan Beddoes in the early 1950s. It was approved by Queen Elizabeth II in February 1956.

A malamute dog stands on snow above the shield. The malamute is one of the largest Arctic sled dogs. It symbolizes courage, loyalty, and the northern land. The malamute dog is shown at the top of the coat of arms. Its body is built to pull heavy objects in extreme conditions, indicating that strength is more important than speed.

Beneath the wreath is the shield. The Cross of St. George occupies the top part of the shield. This cross represents English explorers. The symbol in the centre of the cross is called a "roundel in vair," which stands for the fur trade. The red triangles in the bottom part of the shield represent the territory's mountains. The gold circles inside the triangles are a symbol of the minerals found in these mountains. The wavy white and blue stripes between the red triangles represent the Yukon River and the Klondike creeks where gold was discovered.

Guide to Coats of Arms

THE NATIONAL COAT OF ARMS

ALBERTA

BRITISH COLUMBIA

MANITOBA

NEW BRUNSWICK

NEWFOUNDLAND AND LABRADOR

NORTHWEST TERRITORIES

NOVA SCOTIA

NUNAVUT

ONTARIO

PRINCE EDWARD ISLAND

QUEBEC

SASKATCHEWAN

YUKON

Canada's Coat of Arms

National emblems are symbols that are used for the entire country. The Canadian flag, known as the Maple Leaf, is one such symbol. Another is the common loon, which is the national bird. The maple is the national tree. Canada's national coat of arms represents the country's heritage, land, and people.

Canada's coat of arms is used on official documents and by government offices.

Canada's coat of arms has similar features to that of Great Britain. However, maple leaves have been added. The coat of arms also shows Canada's ties to France.

The country's first official coat of arms was drawn by Mrs. Cathy Bursey-Sabourin in 1921. In 1994, a ribbon with the motto of the Order of Canada was added behind the shield.

Coat of Arms History

Following Confederation, Great Britain's coat of arms was used to represent Canada. A seal depicting each of the four provinces that originally made up the country was approved on May 26, 1968. Over time, it was used as the coat of arms. As more provinces joined the union, they were added. However, the design became cluttered. The Canadian government asked Great Britain for permission to create an official coat of arms. It was formally assigned in 1921.

Parts of the Coat of Arms

Canada's national coat of arms is among the most symbolically important emblems in the country.

SHIELD The shield features Canada's four founding nations. They are England, Scotland, Ireland, and France. The three lions represent the country's ties to England. The red lion represents Scotland. The golden harp represents Ireland. The fleur-de-lis represents France. The three maple leaves are a symbol of Canada.

MOTTO The motto on the ribbon below the shield says *A Mari usque ad Mare*. This means "From Sea to Sea."

THE CROWN The crown shows that the monarch is Canada's head of state. This crown has been used in the **coronation** of British kings and queens for hundreds of years.

CREST The crest is above the royal helmet. It consists of a lion standing on a red and white wreath. This lion, which symbolizes valour and courage, wears the royal crown and holds a maple leaf in its right paw. The crest represents Canada's **sovereignty**.

SUPPORTERS The lion on one side of the shield represents England. The unicorn on the other side represents Scotland.

Test Your Knowledge

1 What is a coat of arms?

4 What country does the fleur-de-lis represent?

2 What does *je me souviens* mean?

5 What animal is used to show Scotland on Canada's coat of arms?

3 Who gave Prince Edward Island its coat of arms?

6 Who were the Beothuk?

7 What is Canada's national animal?

8 When was Saskatchewan's coat of arms approved?

MULTIS E GENTIBUS VIRES

9 What do the wavy white and blue stripes on the Yukon coat of arms represent?

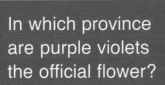

13 In which province are purple violets the official flower?

14 Who was Saint Andrew?

10 How is the crown on Canada's coat of arms used?

15 What animals are shown on Nunavut's coat of arms?

11 Which province has Canada's oldest coat of arms?

12 What does the bear on Ontario's coat of arms represent?

Answers:
1. a special design that represents a group or a region
2. "I remember"
3. King Edward VII
4. France
5. a unicorn
6. Aboriginal Peoples who lived in Newfoundland when Europeans first arrived
7. the beaver
8. September 16, 1986
9. the Yukon River and the Klondike creeks
10. in the coronation of kings and queens for hundreds of years
11. Nova Scotia
12. the abundance of Ontario's varied wildlife
13. New Brunswick
14. the patron saint of Scotland
15. a caribou and a narwhal

 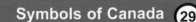

Create Your Own Coat of Arms

Create a coat of arms to represent your family. Begin by thinking about your family's history. Use this book to help you. You may want to include your favorite sports, colours, and flowers. Is there a quote your family uses often? This could become your motto.

Think about how your coat of arms will look. Will it have a shield or banner? Will it include animals? How will you arrange the items on your shield? Why? Look at the pictures in this book for help.

Draw your coat of arms on a piece of paper. Use the diagram on pages 26 and 27 to help you design the parts of your coat of arms. Colour your drawing with felt markers. When you are finished, label the parts of your coat of arms.

Write a description of your coat of arms. What does each item or colour represent? What does it say about you?

Further Research

Many books and websites provide information on coats of arms. To learn more about coats of arms, borrow books from the library, or surf the Internet.

Books

Most libraries have computers that connect to a database for researching information. If you input a key word, you will be provided with a list of books in the library that contain information on that topic. Nonfiction books are arranged numerically, using their call number. Fiction books are organized alphabetically by the author's last name.

Websites

Find fun facts about each of Canada's provinces and territories at **www.pco-bcp.gc.ca/aia/index.asp?lang=eng&page=provterr&sub=map-carte&doc=map-carte-eng.htm**.

Learn about Canada's coat of arms and other symbols at **www.patrimoinecanadien.gc.ca/pgm/ceem-cced/symbl/index-eng.cfm**.

To create a digital coat of arms, visit **www.imaginon.org/fun/whippingboy/createacoatofarms.asp**.

Glossary

allies: people or countries that cooperate with each other on a certain activity

boreal: northern regions with very cold temperatures

colony: a country or area that is ruled by another country

Confederation: the joining together of the provinces to form Canada

coronation: a ceremony in which a king or queen is crowned

First Nations: Canada's first inhabitants, or Aboriginal Peoples, with the exception of Inuit and Métis

heritage: traditions, customs, and ideas that are handed down from earlier generations

inukshuk: a human-like stone figure

migratory: to move from one place to another

Mi'kmaq: the earliest known inhabitants of Prince Edward Island

monarchy: a nation ruled by a royal family

qulliq: an Inuit stone lamp

Royal Crest: a symbol of British royalty

shield: a wide piece of metal or wood that is used as protection

sovereignty: the power of a nation, group, or individual to govern itself

stylized: shown in an unrealistic manner

tundra: vast, treeless land where the ground is always frozen

Index